A Little Book of Love and Companionship

A Little Book of Love and Companionship

Ruskin Bond

SPEAKING TIGER PUBLISHING PVT. LTD
4381/4 Ansari Road, Daryaganj,
New Delhi–110002, India

ISBN: 978-93-86050-39-7
eISBN: 978-93-86050-37-3

10 9 8 7 6 5 4 3 2 1

Typeset in Garamond Pro by SÜRYA, New Delhi
Printed at Thomson Press, Delhi

Introduction

When we are in love we usually burst into song, even if we don't sing very well. No wonder the world's most popular songs and arias—both operatic and pop—tell of love, requited or unrequited; of moonlight serenades, broken hearts, lovers united, lovers parted; of Romeo and Juliet, Laila and Majnun, Heer and Ranjha, Daphnis and Chloe.... The list of great lovers, star-crossed or blessed with happiness, is endless. And so are the singers and songs, from Noor Jehan in *Jugnu*, to Richard Tauber singing 'Love's Last

Word Is Spoken', to Michael Jackson wooing his ecstatic fans with song and sinuous dance.

I'm afraid it doesn't work when I sing. I am usually told to shut up. However, the crows don't seem to mind. Whenever I sing, they gather outside my window and join in the chorus. When they have all left, one remains, its head cocked to one side, looking at me with frank affection. I have no idea if my crow is male or female; obviously my singing transcends these trifles.

But this little book is not just about romantic love. Harmony in people is as beautiful as it is in music, and harmony between two people is the outcome of companionship. 'Love at first sight' may be a many-splendoured thing, but it can as easily vanish at a second sighting. Sometimes true love can take a long time coming to perfect fruition; but when it does, it's there to stay. And that's companionship—adjusting to each other's temperament, learning to live together in perfect harmony.

There are many kinds of love. We love our children, of course. There is nothing equal to a mother's love for the child she has carried, the child she has nourished, the child who has grown before her into a beautiful man or woman. Every child is beautiful. And there is beauty in the abandoned animal, the neglected flower, the little stream, the mighty ocean or mountain range. Anything can be an object of our love. Or should be.

Sometimes I can't help feeling that our dear old planet is on the verge of self-destruction. We have defied both God and Nature, and have created horrific weapons of destruction. Only love can save us. Love for leaf and bud, love for this earth and all that grows and lives upon it. Love for all humanity. Yes, and even love for that handsome black jungle crow who is winking at me from the window.

Ruskin Bond
June 2016

If I am not for myself
Who will be for me
And if I am not for others
What am I?
And if not now, when?

— Hillel the Elder

''Twas my one Glory—
Let it be
Remembered
I was owned of Th ee.'
—*Emily Dickinson*

We must love someone.
We must keep loving all our days,
Someone, anyone, anywhere.
There must be someone
To take your hand
And share the torrid day.
Without the touch of love
There is no life,
and we must fade away.

Through a long period of struggle when I was young, nothing changed. There were days and there were nights, and all the days and nights were the same. A few things reassured me: the desire to love and be loved. Sometimes my love was an exploration of all that is physical; and sometimes it became an exploration of the mind. Love brought me ashore.

We don't know why the world
was made or why we are here.
We are all refugees, and our
only duty is to be each other's
shelter, each other's refuge,
each other's help.

'Love is not in our choice
but in our fate.'
—*John Dryden*

‘In the end there is no desire so deep as the simple desire for companionship.’

—Graham Greene

‘I want someone to sit beside after the day’s pursuit and all its anguish, after its listening, and its waiting, and its suspicions. After quarrelling and reconciliation I need privacy—to be alone with you, to set this hubbub in order.’

—Virginia Woolf

'How should we like it were
stars to burn
With a passion for us we could
not return?
If equal affection cannot be
Let the more loving one be me.'
—W.H. Auden

'Of all forms of caution, caution in love is perhaps the most fatal to true happiness.'
—Bertrand Russell

'Between me and You,
there is only me.
Take away the me,
so only You remain.'
—*Mansur al-Hallaj*

'We were together.
I forget the rest.'
—*Walt Whitman*

The first rule of love is that we should shed our ego. That is also the last rule of love.

'Love is a better teacher
than duty.'
—*Albert Einstein*

‘The garden of love is green
without limit
and yields many fruits other than
sorrow or joy.
Love is beyond either condition:
without spring, without autumn,
it is always fresh.’

—Rumi

‘If nothing saves us from death,
at least love should save us
from life.’

—Pablo Neruda

.Ruskin Bond.

.Ruskin Bond.

.Ruskin Bond.

Except in you I have no rest.

— Dom Moraes

'Time was away and somewhere else,
There were two glasses and two chairs
And two people with one pulse.'

—Louis MacNeice

'"What? You too? I thought I was the only one."...And instantly they stand together in an immense solitude.'

—*C.S. Lewis*

'Come, let's be a comfortable couple and take care of each other! How glad we shall be that we have somebody we are fond of always, to talk to and sit with.'

—*Charles Dickens*

In moments of rare intimacy two people are of one mind and one body, speaking only in thoughts, brilliantly aware of each other, whether they stand arm in arm or apart in a crowded room.

'I am in your clay.
You are in my clay.'
—*Guan Daosheng*

The most lasting relationships are usually those that have grown slowly, without fret or frenzy. Passion is nice to experience, but the important thing is to be comfortable with someone, and not have to keep proving yourself in one way or another.

'Friendship is a sheltering tree.'

—*Samuel Taylor Coleridge*

'It's a strange thing to discover and to believe that you are loved when you know that there is nothing in you for anybody but a parent or God to love.'

—*Graham Greene*

'We don't love qualities, we love people; sometimes by reason of their defects as well as of their qualities.'

—*Th omas Mann*

'It is a curious thought,
but it is only when you see
people looking ridiculous that
you realize just how much you
love them.'

—*Agatha Christie*

'It doesn't matter who you are
or what you look like, so long as
somebody loves you.'

—*Roald Dahl*

'What greater thing is there for two human souls, than to feel that they are joined for life–to strength each other in all labour, to rest on each other in all sorrow, to minister to each other in silent unspeakable memories at the moment of the last parting?'

—*George Eliot*

'Your face, your mouth, your shoulders...Where did they go?... Come home. Do you hear? My lungs are thick with the smoke of your absence.'

—*Raymond Carver*

'Again and again, even though
we know love's landscape
And the little churchyard with its
lamenting names
And the terrible reticent gorge in
which the others end:
Again and again the two of us
walk out together
Under the ancient trees, lay
ourselves down again and again
Among the flowers, and look up
into the sky.'

—*Rainer Maria Rilke*

There are few comforts greater than the touch of a loving hand when your hopes have been dashed.

On lonely nights, even a crazy bat is company.

Who could refrain that had a heart
to love and in that heart
courage to make love known?

— William Shakespeare

'Love has no time for blasphemy
or faith,
Nor lovers for the self, that
feeble wraith.'
—*Farid-ud-Din Attar*

'...I composed a letter to you in the sleepless nightmare hours of the night, and it has all gone: I just miss you, in a quite simple desperate human way. You, with all your undumb letters, would never write so elementary a phrase as that, perhaps you wouldn't even feel it...Damn you, spoilt creature; I shan't make you love me any more by giving myself away like this—But oh my dear, I can't be clever and stand-offish with you: I love you too much for that...you have broken down my defences. And I don't really resent it.'

—*Vita Sackville-West*

‘I like not only to be loved, but also to be told that I am loved. I am not sure that you are of the same mind. But the realm of silence is large enough beyond the grave. Th is is the world of light and speech, and I shall take leave to tell you that you are very dear.’

—*George Eliot*

‘It is better to lose your pride with someone you love rather than to lose that someone you love with your useless pride.’

—*John Ruskin*

'You know what I am going to say. I love you. What other men may mean when they use that expression, I cannot tell; what I mean is, that I am under the influence of some tremendous attraction which I have resisted in vain, and which overmasters me.'

—*Charles Dickens*

'I had to touch you with my hands,
I had to taste you with my tongue;
one can't love and do nothing.'

—*Graham Greene*

'When I give I give myself.'

—*Walt Whitman*

'Each friend represents a world in us, a world possibly not born until they arrive, and it is only by this meeting that a new world is born.'

—*Anais Nïn*

'To love at all is to be vulnerable. Love anything and your heart will be wrung and possibly broken. If you want to make sure of keeping it intact you must give it to no one, not even an animal...Lock it up safe in the casket or coffin of your selfishness. But in that casket, safe, dark, motionless, airless, it will change. It will not be broken; it will become unbreakable, impenetrable, irredeemable.'

—*C.S. Lewis*

'Above all, don't lie to yourself. The man who lies to himself and listens to his own lie comes to a point that he cannot distinguish the truth within him, or around him, and so loses all respect for himself and for others. And having no respect he ceases to love.'

—*Fyodor Dostoyevsky*

In love and friendship it should not matter who yields first.

.Ruskin Bond.

And hand in hand, on the edge of the sand,
They danced by the light of the moon.

— Edward Lear

'Here with a Loaf of Bread
beneath the Bough,
A flask of wine,
a book of verse—and thou
Beside me singing in the
wilderness—
And wilderness is Paradise now.'
—*Omar Khayyam*

'Think of two people, living together day after day, year after year, in this small space, standing elbow to elbow cooking at the same small stove, squeezing past each other on the narrow stairs… jogging, jostling, bumping against each other's bodies by mistake or on purpose, sensually, aggressively, awkwardly, impatiently, in rage or in love—think what deep though invisible tracks they must leave everywhere behind them!'

—*Christopher Isherwood*

'To all men I would say how mistaken they are when they think that they stop falling in love when they grow old, without knowing that they grow old when they stop falling in love.'

—*Gabriel Garcia Márquez*

'Grow old with me!
The best is yet to be.'

—*Robert Browning*

'Come, my Celia, let us prove
While we may, the sports of love;
Time will not be ours forever;
He at length our good will sever.
Spend not then his gifts in vain.
Suns that set may rise again;
But if once we lose this light,
'Tis with us perpetual night.'

—Ben Jonson

'To get the full value of joy you must have someone to divide it with.'

—*Mark Twain*

'There's a kinship among men who have sat by a dying fire and measured the worth of their life by it.'

—*William Golding*

Below my cottage was a forest, and in it, a stream. I went there every day, and slowly the birds and animals accepted me. They grew accustomed to my face. A spotted fork-tail, which at first used to fly away at my approach, now remained perched on a boulder, continually wagging its tail. One day I walked into the stream, and he hopped in too. And we stood together in the cool running water.

And down there, below the old cottage where I grew into middle age, is my old friend, a short Himalayan blue pine now lit by a full moon. For years I sat beneath it to listen to the wind playing softly in its branches. I must walk down there again someday, for it is good to visit old friends.

'The mountains are calling and I must go.'

—John Muir

One is very crazy when in love.

— Sigmund Freud

'Ah me! Love cannot
be cured by herbs.'
—*Ovid*

'Listen, friend, I'm heart-sick!
And the witch-doctor's lost
his mind
He tells me this pain is pleasure!'
—*Anonymous*

'Will you love me in December
as you do in May,
Will you love me in the good
old-fashioned way?
When my hair has all turned grey,
Will you kiss me then and say,
That you love me in December
as you do in May?'

—*Jimmy Walker*

'You must learn to forgive a man when he's in love. He's always a nuisance.'

—*Rudyard Kipling*

You cannot make someone love you. There is no science to it, no formula of success, no black magic charm. All that you can do is to love, and be grateful when it is reciprocated. When I was young, I fell in love with someone, someone fell in love with me and both loves were unrequited. I was very heart-sick for a while; I wrote long letters and poems! Then life carried on, as it usually does. (And yes, I loved again!)

'How little I thought, a year ago,
In the horrible cottage upon the Lee
That he and I should be sitting so
And sipping a cup of camomile tea.

. . .

We might be fifty, we might be five,
So snug, so compact, so wise are we!
Under the kitchen-table leg
My knee is pressing against his knee.'

—*Katherine Mansfield*

'I'm a kafir, a pagan, I worship Love,
I have no need of Islam.
Kafir's wear their sacred thread,
I have no need of that, either.
I'm drunk on the nectar of Love.
He sings
In my blood: each vein a thread
of my faith.'

—*Amir Khusro*

'Love is the beloved, Love the
lover, too;
Love has no time for anything
but Love.'
—*Meer Taqi Meer*

'Wine comes in at the mouth
And love comes in at the eye;
That's all we shall know for truth
Before we grow old and die.
I lift the glass to my mouth,
I look at you, and I sigh.'
—*William Butler Yeats*

'I have felt cats rubbing their faces against mine and touching my face with claws carefully sheathed. These things, to me, are expressions of love.'

—James Herriot

'You know, the way love can change a fellow is really frightful to contemplate.'

—P.G. Wodehouse

.Ruskin Bond.

.Ruskin Bond.

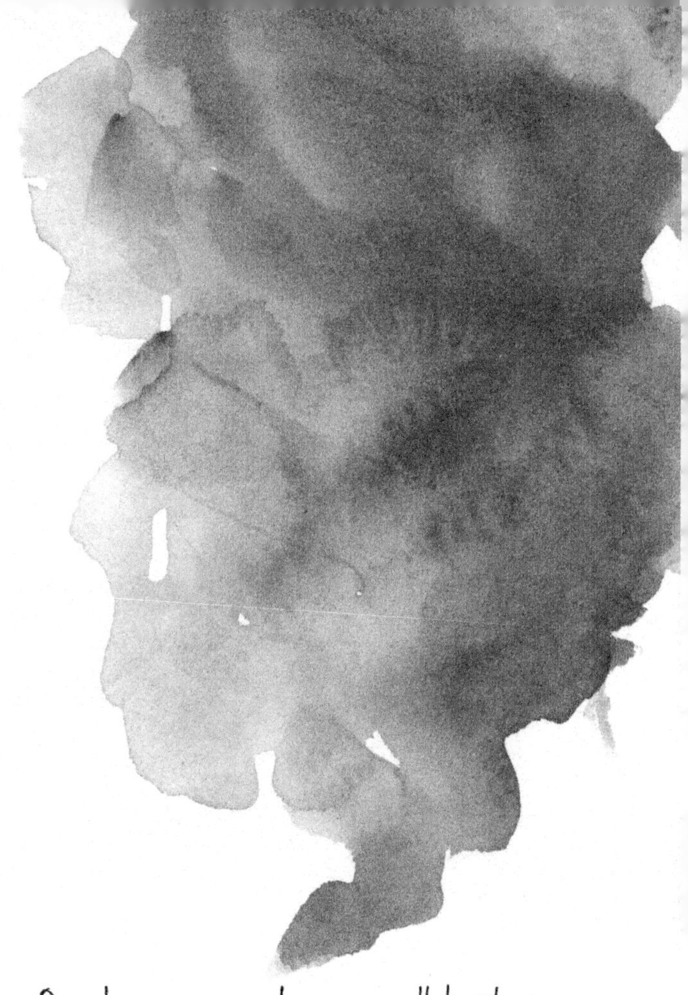

On the open road we are all brothers.

The brush of a stranger's hand on the street and the evening is beautiful, no longer lonely.

'It is good to love the unknown.'
—*Charles Lamb*

'No one is useless in this world who lightens the burden of another.'

—Charles Dickens

'Mighty proud I am that I am able to have a spare bed for my friends.'

—Samuel Pepys

'Give me a companion of my way, be it only to mention how the shadows lengthen as the sun declines.'

—*William Hazlitt*

'No friendship is an accident.'

—*O. Henry*

If I make a house in the woods, I am the intruder. So I leave my windows open all day and all night, till I know I am accepted. And gradually, I am. A stag beetle comes in one day, then returns. At night, fireflies circle the room, twinkling at me from floor or wall. A little bat flies in, flies out, comes back and settles upside down at the foot of my bed. Small birds begin to dart in and out of the rooms at various times of the day. A cherry tree taps at my window. I have a family of friends.

A squirrel comes to my window in the rains, when his home in the oak tree gets waterlogged. He climbs onto the dining table looking for tidbits, which he always finds, because I leave them there. Sometimes he stays after he's done, sitting at the other end of the table, twitching his nose and tail, perhaps to give me company.

.Ruskin Bond.

ove is an act of endless forgiveness,
a tender look which becomes a habit.

— Peter Ustinov

'I wonder why God ever bothered to make men, when he had the whole wide beautiful world to himself,' I asked my friend. 'Why did he find it necessary to share it with anyone?'

'Perhaps he felt lonely,' said my friend.

'We are shaped and fashioned by what we love.'

—*Goethe*

We have to accept people as they are if we want to live with them. You cannot take the love and spurn the lover.

‘Love is wiser than wisdom.’
—*Umberto Eco*

'Love is never any better than the lover.'

—*Toni Morrison*

'We must accept or refuse one another as we are. I could tame a hyena more easily than my friend. He is a material which no tool of mine will work.'

—*Henry David Thoreau*

'Do you know what people really want? Everyone, I mean. Everybody in the world is thinking: I wish there was just one other person I could really talk to, who could really understand me, who'd be kind to me. That's what people really want, if they're telling the truth.'

—Doris Lessing

''Tis the privilege of friendship to talk nonsense, and have her nonsense respected.'

—Charles Lamb

'After a while you learn the
subtle difference
Between holding a hand and
chaining a soul,
And you learn that love doesn't
mean leaning
And company doesn't mean
security.'

—Jorge Luis Borges

'Th e way to love anything is to realize that it may be lost.'

—G.K. Chesterton

'The beginning of love is the will to let those we love be perfectly themselves, the resolution not to twist them to fit our own image. If in loving them we do not love what they are, but only their potential likeness to ourselves, then we do not love them: we only love the reflection of ourselves we find in them.'

—Thomas Merton

'It's nobody's fault that our hearts
work in their little strange ways.
It's nobody's fault that we fall for
one another.
It's nobody's fault that we can't
have the love we yearn.
It's nobody's fault that we never
learn.
So, save your apology, my dear.
Save it for later days. Save it for
better days.'

—Noor Iskandar

ast night, lost memories of you returned—
s spring steals into a wilderness,
s the morning breeze blows gently into a desert,
s relief comes to a sick man for no reason.

Faiz Ahmad Faiz

The years pass. We move on, make new attachments. But sometimes we hanker for the old times, the old friendships, the old loves. I may have stopped loving you, my friends, but I'll never stop loving the days I loved you.

.Ruskin Bond.

An old love—a distant memory now, but a bright one, like a forget-me-not blooming on a bare rock.

❧

'If you love a flower that lives on a star, it is sweet to look at the sky at night. All the stars are a-bloom with flowers...'

—Antoine de Saint-Exupéry

❧

'A man without love, what is
courtesy to him?
A man without love, what is
music to him?'

—*Confucius*

'I don't want to be alone,
I want to be left alone.
There's a difference.'

—*Audrey Hepburn*

You find love when you least expect to, and lose it when you are sure that it is in your grasp. And there are times when it is better to let go than to hold on.

Love may be inconstant,
but it is good to love.

Strangers, briefly met, who became more intimate than friends. I wonder what became of them. Some of the moving forces of our lives are meant to touch us briefly and then go their way.

'I want to know you moved and breathed in the same world as me.'

—F. Scott Fitzgerald

There was a brook at the bottom of the hill. From where I lived I could always hear its murmur, and after some time I was no longer conscious of the sound. And yet, whenever I went away on some journey I felt bereft. Then the journey was over, I returned to my house on the hill, to the murmuring of the brook, and I was no longer lonely.

I know you'll come
When the cherries
Are ripe;
But it is still November
And I must wait
For the green fruit to blush
At your approach.

'Let us be grateful to the people who make us happy; they are the gardeners who make our souls blossom.'

—*Marcel Proust*

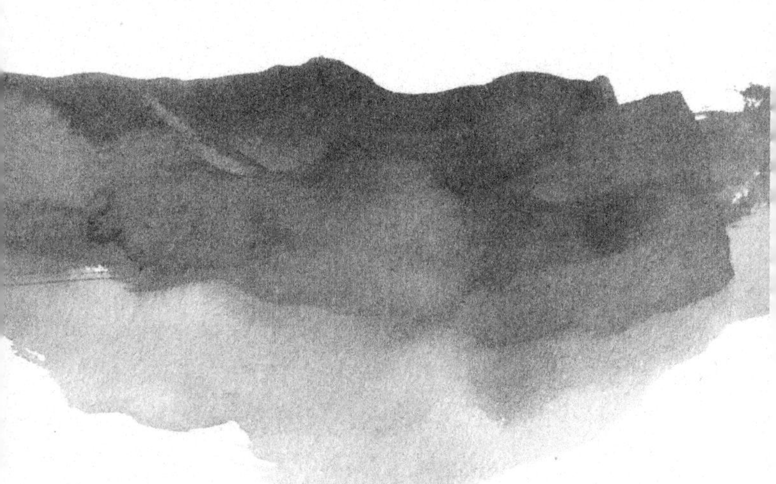

Love tells us, humming,
that the stalled motor
of the heart
has started to work
again.

— Vladimir Mayakovsky

'Sometimes, in the desert
of desire
Caravans halt briefly—
Words, half-said, of love;
Illusions of union.'
—*Faiz Ahmad Faiz*

'Will it last?' asks K. 'Will it last, this feeling of love between us?'

'*This* won't last. Not in this way,' I reply. 'But if something *like* it lasts, we should be happy.'

Two pieces of driftwood come together, and finding themselves caught in the same current, move along with it until they are trapped in a counter-current, and dispersed. A short journey. But it will never be forgotten.

‘I love you,’ you say and it has been said many million times before. ‘I will work for you, stay by you and make you happy, always,’ you say and this too has been said before. You are in no way different from anyone else. And yet these are the only words to say, nothing can mean more, nothing is simpler, nothing can be made to mean more.

'...my words become stained
with your love.
You occupy everything, you
occupy everything.'
—*Pablo Neruda*

'There is no remedy for love but
to love more.'
—*Henry David Thoreau*

'How shall I hold on to my soul,
so that
it does not touch yours? How
shall I lift
it gently up over you on to other
things?
I would so very much like to
tuck it away
among long lost objects in the dark
...
And yet everything which
touches us, you and me,
takes us together like a single bow,
drawing out from two strings but
one voice.
On which instrument are we strung?
And which violinist holds us in
the hand?'

— *Rainer Maria Rilke*

‘Love does not claim possession
but gives freedom.’
—*Rabindranath Tagore*

Enough for me that you are
beautiful.
Enough for me that you walk past,
A firefly flashing in the dark.

‘Lay your sleeping head, my love
Human on my faithless arm;
Time and fevers burn away
Individual beauty from
Thoughtful children, and the grave
Proves the child ephemeral;
But in my arms till break of day
Let the living creature lie:
Mortal, guilty, but to me
The entirely beautiful.’

—*W.H. Auden*

All, everything that I understand,
I understand only because I love.

— Leo Tolstoy

'No man can be called friendless who has God and the companionship of good books.'
—*Elizabeth Barrett Browning*

A mountain stream is the most comforting of friends. Once you have lived with it, and come to know of it, you will find it is always there to listen to your thoughts and share your solitude.

'My Beloved is the mountains,
And lovely wooded valley,
Strange islands,
And resounding rivers,
The whistling of love-stirring
breezes,
The tranquil night
At the time of the rising dawn,
Silent music...'

—John of the Cross

‘Only he whose garment is rent
by the violence of love
Is wholly pure, free of
greed and sin.
Hail, then, O Love,
sweet madness!
You healer of all our ills and
infirmities,
The physician of our pride and
self-conceit.’

—*Rumi*

'O Divine Master, grant that I
may not
Seek to be consoled as to console;
To be understood as to understand;
To be loved as to love;
For it is in giving that we receive,
It is in pardoning that we
are pardoned.'
—*Francis of Assisi*

When I open the window at night, there is always something to listen to: the mellow whistle of a pygmy owlet, or the sharp cry of a barking deer, the sound of a flute from another hill. Sometimes, I see the moon coming up over the next mountain. Who says the world is a lonely place?

'Time spent with a cat is never wasted.'

—*Colette*

'Kindness, I've discovered, is everything in life.'

—*Isaac Bashevis Singer*

'If we have no peace, it is because we have forgotten that we belong to each other.'

—*Mother Teresa*

'Go into your heart, it is the
greatest pilgrimage.
One heart is better than a
thousand Kaabas.'

—*Rumi*

'Love is God, as God is Love
itself;
The two are one, like sun and
sunshine.'

—*Ras Khan*

eing deeply loved by someone gives you strength,
nd loving someone deeply gives you courage.

— Lao Tzu

‘Every heart sings a song, incomplete, until another heart whispers back. Those who wish to sing always find a song. At the touch of a lover, everyone becomes a poet.’

—*Plato*

'There are several kinds of love. One is a mean, grasping, egotistical thing which uses love for self-importance...The other is an outpouring of everything good in you—of kindness and consideration and respect—not only the social respect of manners but the greater respect which is recognition of another person as unique and valuable. The first kind can make you sick and small and weak but the second can release in you strength, and courage and goodness and even wisdom you didn't know you had.'

—John Steinbeck

'Keep love in your heart. A life without it is like a sunless garden when the flowers are dead.'

—*Oscar Wilde*

'Love is like a friendship caught on fire. In the beginning a flame, very pretty, often hot and fierce, but still only light and flickering. As love grows older, our hearts mature and our love becomes as coals, deep-burning and unquenchable.'

—*Bruce Lee*

'Trust your heart if the seas
catch fire,
live by love though the stars
walk backward.'
—E.E. Cummings

'A kiss makes the heart young
again and wipes out all the years.'
—Rupert Brooke

'It isn't possible to love and part. You will wish that it was. You can transmute love, ignore it, muddle it, but you can never pull it out of you. I know by experience that the poets are right: love is eternal.'

—*E.M. Forster*

'Tell your friend that in his death, a part of you dies and goes with him. Wherever he goes, you also go. He will not be alone.'

—*J. Krishnamurti*

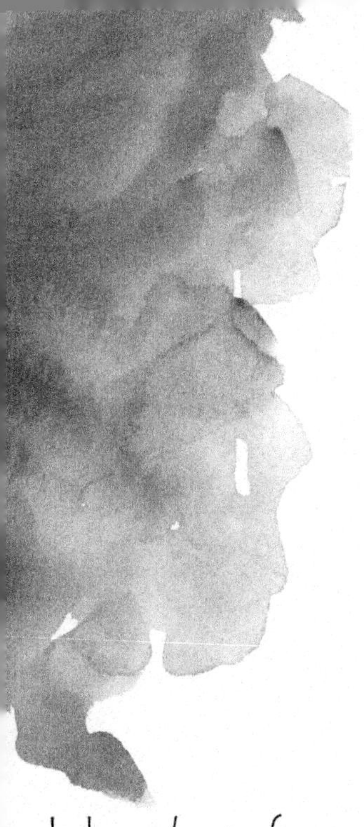

I have learned not to worry about love,
but to honour its coming with all my heart.

— Alice Walker

'What fools we are, eh? What fools, sitting here in the sun, singing. And of love, too! I am too old for it, and you are too young, and yet we waste our time singing about it. Ah well, let's have a glass of wine, eh?'

—*Gerald Durrell*

'The heart wants what it wants.
There's no logic to these things.
You meet someone and you fall
in love and that's that.'

—*Woody Allen*

'What is done in love is well done.'

—*Vincent Van Gogh*

'The happiness of life is made up of minute fractions—the little, soon forgotten charities of a kiss or a smile, a kind look or heartfelt compliment.'

—Samuel Taylor Coleridge

There are always people and things to live for.

'To love or have loved, that is enough. Ask nothing further. There is no other pearl to be found in the dark folds of life.'

—*Victor Hugo*

Every time I look at the night sky I'm aware of belonging to the universe. There are worlds beyond this and they are all mine, as I am theirs. Life is eternal and infinite. We are never alone.

'Gentle lady, do not sing
Sad songs about the end of love;
Lay aside sadness and sing
How love that passes is enough.'

—James Joyce

'As for life's tragedies, our love will defeat them.'

—Naguib Mahfouz

'I know of only one duty, and that is to love.'

—*Albert Camus*

Ruskin Bond is the author of numerous novellas, short-story collections and non-fiction books, many of them classics. Among them are *The Room on the Roof*, *A Flight of Pigeons*, *The Night Train at Deoli*, *Time Stops at Shamli*, *Landour Days*, *Rain in the Mountains*, *A Book of Simple Living*, *A Little Book of Happiness* and *Friends in Wild Places*. He received the Sahitya Akademi Award in 1993, the Padma Shri in 1999 and the Padma Bhushan in 2014. He lives in Landour, Mussoorie, with his extended family.

CPSIA information can be obtained
at www.ICGtesting.com
Printed in the USA
LVOW04s1137170816
500681LV00024B/500/P